# Brokenness to BETTER

## Part 1: Trials and Tribulations

# A.C. GRACIE

Trilogy Christian Publishers
A Wholly Owned Subsidiary of Trinity Broadcasting Network
2442 Michelle Drive
Tustin, CA 92780

Scripture quotations marked (KJV) taken from The Holy Bible, King James Version. Cambridge Edition: 1769.

10 9 8 7 6 5 4 3 2 1
Library of Congress Cataloging-in-Publication Data is available.
ISBN 979-8-89041-489-2
ISBN (ebook) 979-8-89041-490-8

# SYNOPSIS OF BROKENNESS TO BETTER PART I:

## ENDURING TRIALS AND TRIBULATIONS

---

### Revelation 12:11 (KJV)

*And they overcame him by the blood of the Lamb,
and by the word of their testimony; and they
loved not their lives unto the death.*

---

In *Brokenness to Better,* A.C. Gracie invites you through her journey of faith by sharing the experiences throughout her life that have equipped her to become the woman of God she is today. Her transparency allows others to see the highs and lows throughout her life as a servant and woman of God. Her testimonies can bring healing, encouragement, and hope in the Lord. The Word of God says we are to share our testimonies. There is power in sharing our trials and tribulations with others and not keeping them all to ourselves. Our testimony not only brings glory to God and shows how He's gotten us through but our testimony can also draw others to the Lord because of our experiences.

# Foreword

---

**Genesis 50:20 (KJV)**

*But as for you, ye thought evil against me; but God meant it unto good, to bring to pass, as it is this day, to save much people alive.*

---

A.C. Gracie is a phenomenal mother of two handsome and intelligent sons, Jelani and Christian. I have watched her walk this thing called life out for over ten years. I am extremely impressed with her desire to open the doors to her personal hurt, trauma, disrespect, and pain she has endured over her forty-plus years of living. This book is a must read for all people. It will set the captives free and liberate those who have lived in an emotional prison. Your hearts will be set free as you learn that the horrific abuse she endured as a child and young adult can be uprooted and liberated to enable her to love again. Most importantly, you will learn to love yourself and no longer be the victim of someone's inappropriate behavior towards your innocence.

**Dr. James H. Kithcart**
*Divine Eternity Fellowship International,*
*Mountain Top Ministries International*

# Dedication

*This book is dedicated to HIM who has been with me all the days of my life, even through all the highs and lows, and to those seeking to know HIM.*

# Acknowledgements

This book would not have been possible without the nudging of the Holy Spirit, my spiritual leaders, and His plan for my life. The experiences that I went through as a child all the way up to adulthood have strengthened me. The trauma, hurt, pain, embarrassment, and humiliation as well as the blessings throughout my journey have made me a better person, mother, and more importantly a servant and a child of God.

I am so very grateful for my children, Jelani and Christian. These words really cannot express how much I love you both. God fulfilled my dream of becoming a mother when He blessed me with the two of you. I thank you both for enduring with me during the highs and lows of my life. I truly appreciate the encouragement you both gave me. Please know that you were the fuel I needed to continue on this journey no matter what I experienced. I look forward to continuing to watch you grow into the young men God has called you to be as well as pursue your dreams.

To my mother, or Momma as I call you, I thank you for everything you have done for me and my children. In my opinion, you've done an outstanding job with the cards you were dealt throughout your life. I am extremely proud that you are my momma and I love you dearly. I love my siblings with all my heart. Every single one of you has played a part in my growth and taught me many different lessons along the way. Rufus, my baby brother, I love you. A day doesn't pass without me thinking of you. You'll forever be in my heart.

To every teacher, pastor, apostle, evangelist, and prophet or prophetess that has crossed my path and poured into me and my children, I thank you. Thank you for all the encouragement you've given me along my spiritual journey. I thank those of you who have labored and endured with me as I have grown into the things of God and found my path that He has laid out for me. Thank you for your patience with me and commitment to doing the work of the Lord.

Thank you to my mentor, Dr. Mildred Ware-Scott. You have been a blessing to me and my young men and I just want to thank you again for all that you've done for us. Thank you for the guidance, prayers, and encouragement. I love you. To all those I consider friends, thank you for accepting me. To strangers that have crossed my path and poured into me out of the blue, I thank you.

# Introduction

I am forty-seven years old. I have never been married. I am a single mother of two children—two wonderful young men. I am a military veteran who served honorably in the United States Air Force. More importantly, I am a servant and child of God.

As a young girl, I dreamt of pursuing my education and getting married. I knew I was going to get a college education. There was never any doubt in my mind about that. I desired the husband, the children, and the house with a white picket fence, with a two-car garage. No, I never considered pets because I never wanted any pets. I also believed that marriage would happen.

I experienced childhood trauma as well as trauma while serving on active duty. Both have negatively affected my relationships. I wasn't aware of it during the time of these relationships. However, I know that now. I am doing what I need to do to overcome all that trauma.

As I got older and started to have intimate relationships, I began to worry about not being married. I started to think that I was not worthy of being a wife or to be married. To be honest, I really didn't know my worth as a woman and a child of God. I was comfortable in those relationships because I had someone. Being coupled up made me feel comfortable even though the relationship may have been unhealthy. After I found out I was pregnant with my first child, I started pursuing the Lord.

While pursuing the Lord and going through the storms of life, I eventually began to see my worth as a woman of God. I began to evaluate those past intimate relationships where I longed to be married. In time, God revealed to me why those the relationships ended. The journey has been painful and extremely uncomfortable at times, but has also been a blessing. The entire journey has prepared me for a moment such as this.

I decided to write this book a few months ago despite receiving word back in 2011 to write it. The decade-long delay was due to the fact that I wasn't ready to expose my truth. I was scared and afraid. I first had to confront the truth and deal with it mentally and spiritually before I could share the experiences that occurred in my life.

We have all experienced hurt, pain, triumph, and maybe some sort of trauma in our lives. I am hoping that the experiences revealed in this book are relatable. We all go through things, good and bad. I hope you're able to see that I did not make it through by myself but with God and those He sent to help me along the way.

# Table of Contents

# My Beginning

---

**Isaiah 41:10 (KJV)**

*Fear thou not; for I am with thee: be not dismayed;
for I am thy God: I will strengthen thee; yea, I will
help thee; yea, I will uphold thee with the right
hand of my righteousness.*

---

I grew up in a single parent home with four siblings. I have two older sisters and two younger brothers. My sisters were eight and seven years older than me. My brothers were four and seven years younger than me. I am the middle child. My two older sisters have the same father and my two younger brothers have the same father. I am the odd man out, as they say. My momma was a teenage mother who dropped out of school in the ninth grade. My momma did the best she could raising us by herself, and I am truly grateful for her. I used to refer to myself as the "black sheep" of the family and said I was adopted for several years.

Despite not actually being adopted, I am different from my siblings and other family members my age. I have always been introverted, a book worm, and a nerd. When I was younger, I tried to fit in and to follow the crowd. Somewhere along the way, I stopped trying to fit in and just did my own thing. A positive outcome of that is that I wasn't a follower and I didn't do what others did such as drugs or sex.

While some of my relatives and friends were having sex, getting abortions, or doing drugs, I kept myself occupied writing poetry or doing something educational. I immersed myself with educational things as my male cousins were going in and out of juvenile detention for committing crimes or female cousins were getting pregnant as teenagers. I remember going to summer school after my freshman year of high school by taking two classes to gain credit hours sooner. Every summer after that one, I went to pre-college programs at several different colleges in and out of the state of Louisiana. I did that to immerse myself into things away from what everyone else was doing. Plus, education and learning have always been outlets for me as well as a love of mine.

On the other hand, a negative outcome of doing my own thing was that I became sort of a loner and isolated myself. I wanted to hang out with my cousins, but I did not want to get involved in the activities they were doing; so, I kept to myself. I think back on all the poetry I used to write in high school and realize that my poetry was about love and wanting friendships or relationships.

As a child, I longed for love. I knew my momma loved me. She just never said it. Seriously, she never said it. However, she showed me she loved me by taking care of me and providing for me. She displayed her love when she spent her last penny on us kids and she would go without. I know she loved us. However, as a child, I think I needed her to say that she loved me more often. Today, she says it often. I tell her I love her numerous times throughout our conversations. I do it to make her say it back. She will say it initially at times, but I say it several times because I love to hear her response.

Growing up, I longed for a one-on-one relationship with my momma. By the time I was in the fifth grade, my two older sisters were out of high school and off to college or the military. So it was just me and my two younger brothers. My momma worked a lot. While she was at work, we were at my grandparents' house until she got off. As I got older, I was able to stay home alone with my younger brothers when she worked. I never had the opportunity to establish a mother and daughter bond because when she wasn't at work she was resting or out with her friends or siblings doing her own thing away from us kids. I grew up seeing most of my female friends have a close-knit relationship with their mothers. It was something I truly desired but never really had the opportunity to experience.

To present a clearer picture, I did not have a father

figure in my life. I knew of my biological father but did not really know him and he was incarcerated most of my life. My momma was a single parent despite being legally married to a man who was not my father. She dated a few men while I was growing up. One of her boyfriends I distinctively remember was Mr. Jerry. I thought, no, I hoped, that he and my momma would one day get married. He was an educated man and had a really good job at a paper mill company. He was truly the closest thing to a father for me. I remember him being very protective of me. He was even interested in all the nerdy things I would talk about. I also remember his birthday was in March just like mine; actually, it is exactly one week before mine. Unfortunately, Mr. Jerry's life was cut short at the age of 32 as he died suddenly of a massive heart attack. My momma went on to date other men. However, Mr. Jerry had always been in my heart; I still think of him every now and then even though he's been gone since 1990. How do I know? He died when I was in the ninth grade of high school.

Even though my momma dated different men, I had the opportunity to witness a great partnership, relationship, and marriage growing up. My grandparents, my mother's parents, were that couple. I called my grandfather Paw, and my grandmother Muhdeah. I have always been in awe of their marriage, even to this very day as I write this. My grandfather loved my grandmother and it was shown by his actions every day. He was the head of the household. My grandmother never worked a day in her life. My grandfather was the sole provider and he was awesome at it. My grandfather was an entrepreneur and had his own business in their home. He had a store there that sold soda, cookies, pickles, freeze cups, and cigarettes. I can remember as a little kid watching the huge Coca-Cola delivery truck pull up to my grandparents' driveway and haul up all different sorts of Coca-Cola products. His business was very profitable and he took care of his family. I admired my grandparents' marriage and prayed that I would have a marriage like theirs one day. It has not happened yet; however, I have not given up on that dream. It will happen as it's all in God's timing.

At forty-seven years of age, I now realize it took me a long while to get to the place where I currently am in my faith and I still have a long way to go. However, I intend to continue walking along this journey with the hopes of increasing my faith and trust in my Lord and Savior, all the while blessing those who I come in contact with.

As a child, I saw my mother work two and three jobs. I remember seeing her in the mornings when she was getting ready for work. Oftentimes, I didn't see her in the evenings because she got off late and we were usually asleep when she came home. Plenty of time was spent at my grandparents' home until I got old enough to stay at home with two younger brothers. My momma worked hard. She wanted to make sure that we had a roof over our heads, food, and clothes. Seeing my mother work tirelessly to provide for us was the push I needed to pursue my educational goals. I knew at a very young age that I wanted a college education. I felt that a college education was needed in order for me to have one good job. I didn't want to work two or three jobs like my mother. I missed a lot of time with my momma because she was always working when I was growing up. I knew I wanted to have one job so that I could have time for my family, husband, and children.

As I was growing up, there was always my Aunt Cootah! Aunt Cootah (her real name was Joyce) was one of my momma's older sisters. I hate to say this, but she was my favorite aunt. When my momma was at work, sometimes we were at Aunt Cootah's house. Aunt Cootah loved God! She took us to church every chance she got. I remember attending usher board meetings, finance meetings, Bible study, choir practice, Sunday School, and Vacation Bible School. It didn't matter what the church was having or when, Aunt Cootah had us there. Aunt Cootah introduced me to the Lord and she ensured that we knew of Him and the things He had done, did, and would yet do. I got baptized around eight or nine years old by Reverend Green at St. Peter Baptist Church. I remember it like it was yesterday.

One defining moment was a day I was at Aunt Cootah's house. My momma had gotten us ready for church and taken us over there. Well, I decided that I didn't like my hair the way my momma had combed it. So I went to the back room, looked in the mirror, and proceeded to change my hairstyle. Aunt Cootah came up behind me and popped me on my bottom with a belt. She scared me because I didn't see it coming and I rarely got spankings. As I was crying, she turned me around, kneeled down, and said something I have never forgotten. "Leave your hair alone. You are special to God; don't try to fit in with everyone else." At that time, I had no idea what she was saying or meant; however, as time has gone by, I know exactly what she meant. Aunt Cootah passed away when I was 10 years old, soon after my cousin, her daughter and only child, turned 13. After Aunt Cootah passed away, going to church on a regular basis stopped. We would attend, but only when Momma could get us there or if we spent the night with Muhdeah and Paw. I always think of Aunt Cootah. I admired her; she was smart and more importantly, she loved God—someone I was trying to get to know.

From the time I was about four years old to about 12 years of age, I was molested by my momma's male friend. Whenever he came around, he would always put me on his lap and somehow touch my private parts while I was sitting on his lap. There was never sexual intercourse; however, he touched me inappropriately often while others were in the same room as us but were not paying attention. I recall one time while my mother was occupied with another male friend, he sat on a bed, pulled out his private part, spat on it, and made me massage it. I apologize for being so descriptive, but these are the images and memories that I remember.

When I was in the seventh grade, I took gymnastics for physical education. I recalled my teacher, Ms. Clements, discussed sex education. I remembered she told us that no one should be touching you—not your parents, not anyone. She said that if anyone was doing that to us it was wrong and should be reported. As she said that, all sorts of emotions came to the surface. I was sad, angry, and confused. No one had ever told me that no one was supposed to touch me or my private parts. No one ever told me that I was not supposed to be massaging a man's private parts. From that moment on, when he came around, I disappeared. I disappeared to my room with the door locked or went outside. I told myself, *"He will NEVER touch me again"* and he did not. I never told my momma or anyone that I was molested until I was 25 years old, after having my first child.

Eventually, I graduated from high school and left my hometown to attend college. I had earned a five-year academic scholarship to attend any public school in Louisiana. During my freshman year of college, I attended classes as I should but at night I was out seeking love. I only dated a few guys, but, looking back at it, I used my body to attempt to obtain love. I thought having sexual intercourse would lead to love. That was not the case. Sexual intercourse just led to more sexual intercourse.

When I went home for spring break, one day I answered the phone but didn't recognize the voice right away. "Is this Buffy? I heard you're in college now. I know you're screwing everything on that campus." I immediately dropped the phone and told my momma she had a call.

It was that sick man. The man who had inappropriately touched me all those years was on the phone. I could not believe that he was calling my momma. I locked myself in my room for the rest of the week and blocked him out of my mind. I was so lost and frustrated. I registered for the fall semester of my sophomore year of college but never went back to that school. I needed a break and desperately wanted to get away from everything and everyone.

My first real relationship was with a man who was in the military. He was three years older than me. It was convenient for him as he was stationed in one city and I went to college in another. He treated me well but cheated on me often. He and I would date on and off for a few years until he confessed he'd had a one night stand and gotten the woman pregnant. He and I tried to work past that fact, but I could never really trust him again. I was devastated. How could someone say they love you but hurt you and cheat on you constantly? I wondered what I was lacking to make him cheat. I doubted myself and my self-worth. Why wasn't I enough and what did I do wrong? I decided to enlist into the military instead of going back to school. I needed a break and wanted to get away from everything, everyone, and the hurt, and that was the quickest way to do so.

# The Getaway

**Psalm 27:1 (KJV)**

*The LORD is my light and my salvation; whom
shall I fear? The LORD is the strength of my life;
of whom shall I be afraid?*

In 1996, I enlisted in the military. I was off on a new adventure. This was totally different and new to me. This was my chance to get away from my hometown, the people, and all the hurt. After completing basic training and technical school, my first duty station was at Laughlin Air Force Base in Del Rio, Texas. I adjusted to the military well, but for some reason I was often sick at the base. Despite that and the fact that I did not like the location of the base, I liked the people I had an opportunity to meet. Another positive note was that my older sister, ReRe, was four and half hours away stationed at Fort Hood Army Base, so I could visit her often.

Before leaving my first duty station, I ended up getting attacked. To make a long story short, there was this guy who had stolen my dirty panties and was showing them to all the males in the dormitory. Two of the males saw the panties and noticed the initial and last four numbers inscribed on them and realized that all the dirty underwear belonged to me. They told me. I sat there in disbelief of what they told me. I slipped away and confronted the guy in his dorm room. I told him he was a pervert and asked him how he got access to my dirty panties. As I was talking to him, I saw a pair of panties hanging in between his mattresses, pulled them out and saw that they were mine. Suddenly, he attacked me and began to choke me. Thankfully, the two guys figured out where I had disappeared off to, rushed in, and pulled him off me. Of course, I reported it to my supervisor and she convinced me not to report it to military police because I would be leaving the base in a few months to go to my overseas assignment in Okinawa, Japan. I totally suppressed all those memories from 1997-1998 until 2020 and then everything came rushing back like a flood.

In the summer of 1998, I arrived on Okinawa, Japan, to begin working at my new duty station. I was there for over three years. I got pregnant two years after arriving on the island. This is where I met my oldest child's father and where I birthed my first child. Our relationship had been filled with ups and downs. I had a smart mouth and he often drank alcohol and smoked cigarettes. I was excited about becoming a parent but I was disappointed that marriage didn't occur first. However, there was excitement at the possibility of getting married. I told my momma as soon as

I found out. I thought she would be upset because I wasn't married. To my surprise, she was happy about the news. She said I was a responsible adult and that being unwed was not a problem for her. My son's father's family was not sure of me and really did not accept me. There was talk about how the baby should come out with lighter skin if he was really the father. There were issues about me not being light skinned. Things I didn't think would ever be a problem, especially not issues pertaining to skin tone. That alone brought stress into our relationship.

After finding out I was pregnant, I started going to church on base. Before getting pregnant, I went to church sporadically but not often. I went every week, Bible study and even choir practice. When I found out I was going to have a baby, getting to know the Lord became a priority for me. At the time I didn't know why. However, in hindsight I know I needed to have a relationship with God because I truly needed Him and I wanted my children to have a lifestyle that included God in everything. Aunt Cootah popped up in my mind and all the things she'd done came back to me. Plus, the fact of being pregnant in another country thousands of miles away from my momma assured me I needed God. During my first pregnancy, I sought the Lord and started to have a real prayer life. My son's father even went to church with me a few times, but I went faithfully. I was entering a new phase of my life, desiring the Lord's protection, a healthy baby, and praying for marriage to my son's father.

During childbirth, there were many complications. The baby was eight days overdue, and my body would not dilate beyond three and a half centimeters. The baby was in distress and his vitals were plummeting. I got an epidural and had an emergency Cesarean section. When they reached my baby, the umbilical cord was wrapped around his neck. Thank God the baby was healthy, I thought as I heard his cries. The first twelve hours after his birth were so scary. I prayed and prayed because I had no idea what was going on. I was totally numb and could not move nor feel my legs for twelve hours after delivering my baby. All sorts of thoughts ran through my head as I cried. Furthermore, I could not be with my baby until they determined why I had no sensation or feeling in my legs. So, I worried about the mother-baby bond as my baby was with his dad all this time. Immediately, the doctors ran tests and scans on me. No one knew why I didn't have any feeling from my waist down. Many hours after all the tests and scans, I could feel my legs and move them. Doctors and nurses never determined what caused the temporary paralysis. They were all astonished and could not believe that I was up and walking and in no pain the next day after having a Cesarean section. I remember walking down the hallway to go do the paperwork for my baby's birth certificate and passport. The medical staff could not believe I had just had a Cesarean section and continuously asked me if I was all right or in any pain. I thought to myself, *"God was having mercy on me."* That's why I had no pain from the Cesarean section. I thanked Him for His mercy.

After I had my first child, his father received orders to another military installation. Sure, I started worrying as I never thought I would be raising my child by myself, unmarried. I had already been praying to the Lord but then I began asking for a sign to let me know if my baby's father was the man that He had for me. When my baby was four months old, we decided to go visit his family in Maryland for Thanksgiving, and then, my baby and I would go to my hometown shortly after. As my son's father and I began packing, I accidentally knocked over a figurine. It was a statue of a husband hugging his wife with a baby in their arms. Well, the head of the man was the only thing that broke on the figurine. That was my sign. I even asked God if that was my sign when it happened but I brushed if off as not being the sign. To say the least, the trip was horrible. Things occurred that really opened my eyes. As I held my baby in the airport waiting to board the flight to Louisiana, the image of that figurine ran through my mind. In my gut, I knew we weren't going to be together. Needless to say, I still held onto hope that we may end up together.

Eventually I ended up back in Japan with my infant son and my baby's father had moved to Nevada for his next assignment. It was hard being a single parent with my baby's father not being there to help. However, honestly, I enjoyed being a first-time mother. When I became a mother, no, when I became pregnant, I knew I had to be responsible for this little person. I knew I had to take care of my baby with or without his father being there. Luckily, I was able to lean on a couple of God-fearing married women who were there to sort of guide me.

# Dirty And Afraid

---

**Romans 8:1-2 (KJV)**

*There is therefore now no condemnation to them
which are in Christ Jesus, who walk not after the
flesh, but after the Spirit. For the law of the Spirit of
life in Christ Jesus hath made me free from the law
of sin and death.*

---

As I started to have intimate relationships again, the
trauma that occurred in my childhood actually affected
those relationships. I never considered the fact that the
trauma had or could have a negative affect on me in any
way because I was unaware of the trauma in most of my
relationships. I actually suppressed all those memories
pertaining to the molestation. Plus, I had never told anyone,
so it was easier for me to forget and act as if it had never
happened to me. However, little did I know, the trauma
would creep up occasionally.

In intimate relationships, I was shy and afraid of being
naked or even to be seen naked. I would cover myself up

or want the lights totally out. It was as if I was ashamed of myself. Despite being a petite female, I was uncomfortable in my own skin. I wasn't afraid of what my body looked like but was scared of being naked. I was ashamed because I associated nakedness with the molestation and dirtiness. I always felt dirty and really didn't know why I felt that way. In committed relationships, my partners would ask me why I was so scared of being naked. I would shy away from the questions; just thinking about it or talking about it I felt dirty. Those same questions continued to come up and my partner was really concerned about the issue. To be honest, it was difficult to talk about the root cause of me not wanting to be naked.

In my mind, being covered up was my protection. Clothing made me feel more protected. I was more comfortable in the dark. I didn't want to be seen that way. Being naked was a bad thing in my mind. Therefore, I had to cover myself up with clothes, and if I were in bed, I covered myself with the sheets and blankets.

The trauma caused me to have low self-esteem. I didn't think I was good enough for anyone. I didn't think I was worthy to be a wife. At times, I avoided intimacy. I had a history of bad relationships. I was able to share my emotions. I was able to express my emotions about anything and everything but could not expose being molested. I was able to form relationships, but those relationships were broken. Why? Trust. I said I trusted the men but actually I did not trust them at all. So many thoughts ran through my mind. Thoughts of my partner cheating or doing something wrong frequently popped up in my head. Even though the men brought their own issues into the relationship and actually were cheating, my accusations caused problems as well. This happened in all my relationships.

In my dreams, the molestation would show up. A few times, I had nightmares as I slept in the bed next to my partner. Occasionally, I woke up crying, afraid, and distraught as if the abuse was occurring right then and there. My partner would wake up and console me. After years of dating, I finally told my partner. It was by far the hardest thing I had to do. I was humiliated and really didn't understand why it had happened to me. I still don't know. I will never know. However, I was relieved that I had finally told someone. A heavy burden had been lifted. The dreams subsided and I went on living my life as if the trauma had never occurred.

This childhood trauma affected my personality. Throughout school, elementary to high school, I was always a smart student. However, as time passed and I got older, I continued being smart but with an edge. I created a facade. It was a defense mechanism. I tried to be masculine. I cussed like a sailor. Really, I did. I cussed around friends but never at home in the presence of my family. Away from home, I acted as if I was tough and hard—as if nothing bothered me. Only a select few people really knew the real me. I wasn't this small, rough, tough and hard person. I was actually super-sensitive on the inside and very timid.

Along the way, I stopped showing that sensitive and timid side and put on that facade. I was hard on the outside but soft on the inside and that's how Pop Tart became about. Only those close to me knew me as Pop Tart. As I sit here and write this, my male friends were the ones who came up with that name for me. I had female friends; however, I had more male friends than female friends. It wasn't that I could not get along with females. I just did not like all the girly, soft feminine stuff as I didn't want attention brought to me, especially my body. Plus, I realized early on as a child that females tend to have plenty of drama and I had always tried to stay away from that.

For some reason, I always bonded easier with males. I preferred to be the homie or homegirl and not the interesting or attractive girl. I didn't want males to be interested in me. I would prefer to be in the friend zone and maintain platonic relationships with males, and nowhere near the intimate zone. I figured if they were not interested in me I would have no issues with being physical. During my senior year of high school, I started have interest in relationships with males other than platonic relationships but that facade would continue to be around.

After giving birth to my first child, I was extremely protective of my baby. I did not want him to go to daycare. I did not want him out of my sight. I was afraid someone would touch him inappropriately like I had been touched. I thought my baby would be in danger. I wanted to do all that I could to ensure my baby was safe. When my maternity leave was almost complete, I was concerned about leaving my baby at the daycare. Thankfully, I was serving on active duty overseas and all daycare workers had to go through a complete background check before being hired. On top of that, there were cameras in all the rooms all over the facility. If anyone abused any child, it would be caught on camera. That put my mind at ease and gave me the push I needed to enroll my baby into the childcare development center.

When my son was almost two months old, I had a nightmare. The nightmare was about the man that molested me. However, in the dream, he was molesting my baby. That dream really scared me. That dream would be the catalyst to push me to inform my momma of what happened to me. It was extremely hard for me to do. Before I called my momma, I prayed and asked the Lord to help me during the conversation. I had no idea how the conversation would go. All I knew was that I needed to tell my momma. I also wanted to know if that particular man was still around.

I remember standing in my kitchen as I called my momma. I greeted her and asked her how she was doing. She then asked about my baby. I told her he was well but sound asleep. I asked her if she had time as I needed to tell her something very important. I asked her if she was alone. I told her to please go to a room where she was alone and could talk in private. She was anxious. She wanted to know what I had to say. So, when she told me she was in a room by herself, I let it all out. I told her that her friend

(I called him by his nickname) had molested me from about the age of four to twelve years of age. The call went silent. For a moment, I thought she had hung up on me. She asked me if I was serious. She then went on to name other men she had dated and asked if they had touched me inappropriately. I told her there was only one man who had touched me inappropriately and it was specifically that friend of hers. She profusely apologized and asked me why I didn't say something sooner. I told her that I was scared to say something. I didn't think she would believe me. I told her I was saying something now because of the dream I had the night before about my baby. I then asked her if he was still around. I told her that I wanted to contact the local police department there and press charges, and she told me that he was dead. He had died of cancer over a year ago. At first, I was relieved he could no longer violate anyone else; then I wondered if there were other victims like myself.

After returning to the United States, I did not like for my child to be with my own mother at times. Why? I was molested and my mother was in the house with me when the molestation happened. She was in the house every time that man touched me inappropriately. She did not protect me all those years when I was molested. So, I had issues with trusting her with my child. As I write this, my momma still does not know that she was around every time that man touched me in appropriately.

Eventually, I allowed her to babysit my son. She would babysit my son when I was at school as I attended undergraduate classes at night. However, I was calling her every hour, if not every thirty minutes. I did not want anything to happen to my son. So, I checked in to make sure everything was all right with him. I know it probably got on her nerves, but I had to do what I had to do to ensure he was okay.

I continued to be very protective of both of my sons. I did not allow them spend the night at other people's houses. As a matter of fact, they could not go visit other people in their home unless I met the parents and visited the home first. I did what my momma didn't do. I told my children at very young ages that no one was supposed to touch them. I told them both if that ever happened to come to me immediately. I told them I was there to protect them and I would do that with my life for them. I told them I didn't care who it was, to tell me immediately. I told them that frequently. When they both got older and participated in group sports, that conversation was repeated. I wanted to make sure my children had awareness of those types of unfortunate things that happen not only to kids but also adults. I wanted them to be aware of predators and to let me know at all costs if something happened.

# The Getaway Is Over

---

**Psalm 34:17-19 (KJV)**

*The righteous cry, and the Lord heareth, and delivereth them out of all their troubles. The Lord is nigh unto them that are of a broken heart; and saveth such as be of a contrite spirit. Many are the afflictions of the righteous: but the Lord delivereth him out of them all.*

---

Despite giving my all to that relationship, it didn't work out. I got out of the military a year after my baby was born. I decided to end my military career and go back home to complete my education. While I was back in my hometown, I worked full time and attended school full time. My baby was in daycare during the day, and, if I had class in the evening, my momma or baby brother, Rufus, would babysit for me. About six months after leaving Japan, I started getting emails and phone calls from friends back in Japan. They were calling me since they were concerned. All of them said that they had seen a man that looked like my son's father getting married to another woman on MTV.

Of course, I was shocked and concerned. I assured them that he was not married; we hadn't gotten married. After the fifth email and call, I asked him about it, which was in January of that year. He denied it profusely and told me not to be concerned.

Well, four months later, in May, I arrived at my momma's house. I was going to work on some homework in the living room. I got the remote and turned on the television. I was not paying attention to the screen and I heard my son, who was almost two years old at the time, say, "Da Da!" I looked up at the screen and I saw my son's father in a suit holding another woman's hands and they were getting married on MTV by a well-known celebrity. I was totally devastated. I don't even know if that describes it accurately. I was hurt, angry, and confused all at once. My family, mother, sisters, brothers, close friends, could not believe it. I had been asking repeatedly as people from Japan kept contacting me about it and he denied it. He did not respect me enough or care about us enough to tell me the truth. We found out that way. I was embarrassed and humiliated. I went into a deep, deep depression. I wanted to give up on everything, including life. I remember my momma coming to the room, turning on the light and saying, "Buffy, you can't live in the dark and cry forever. You got a baby to take care of!" She was harsh and right at the same time, but I was hurt deeply. I took care of my baby, went to work, went to school, and went to church, but I was broken.

To make things even worse, I found out a few weeks later that not only was he married but he had a newborn baby girl. A couple months after finding out that he was married with a baby, my son's father started to doubt me and my character based on things being told to him by his wife, someone who knew absolutely nothing about me. On our son's second birthday, I had to take my baby and myself to a lab to get our mouths swabbed for a paternity test. My son's father filed a motion with the court stating that he did not think our son was his child. This was a court ordered appointment, one that they scheduled for me and my child. That was a new low for him. I never thought he would go that low but he did, and it brought me down even lower. The results showed that, without a shadow of a doubt, he was and is the father of our son. Having to go through that, and on my child's birthday no less, broke me even further. Through all of this, I asked God, "Why me?"

I shut myself off from everyone. I took my son to daycare, went to work, went to school, picked my son up, attended church, and spent time with my son. Repeat. I saw family, but it was only if they were babysitting my son. I didn't date for over three years, until I met my second child's father. He seemed like a nice guy. He and I really didn't know each other. Just so happened, he was in my hometown because Hurricane Katrina struck New Orleans and he was in town waiting for the hurricane to pass through. Things went fast. He moved in with me and my son. I was yearning for companionship, love, and intimacy. I ignored the red flags that had been shown. I ended up pregnant. Once again, I was excited about the baby and the possibility of getting married. He and I ended up going to the courthouse and getting a marriage license, but it was all for nothing.

During my second pregnancy, my body went into labor when I was four months pregnant. I was hospitalized for a while, then put on bed rest for the duration of the pregnancy. At the time, I was working full time and attending school full time. I went on sick leave at work but eventually went into a leave without pay status at my job. Luckily, it was a federal position and I had a legitimate medical excuse so my job was secure; however, no one donated leave to me so I did not have any income coming in except for my son's child support. I had to withdraw from all my classes as I wasn't able to attend class. My unborn baby's father had a hard time gaining employment because he had a felony on his background that showed up once employers conducted a background check. He was angry and frustrated because he could not get a job. I was upset at myself for not really getting to know him and now I was in this situation. There was friction between us, but I tried to make the best out of it. Being on bed rest for the duration of my pregnancy was hard. I had to go to the doctor three days a week to ensure the baby was okay and that I hadn't dilated any further. I had to be in bed when I was home. So, it was hard as I could not really get up and play with my son. Luckily, he was in pre-kindergarten at the time and my momma helped me out by getting him to and from school as well as daycare whenever he attended.

To make a very long story short, we did not end up together. One day after coming home from the hospital, my best friend came over to pick up a gift for her cousin's baby shower. There was a knock on the door and I answered it. We chatted for a few minutes. She wanted to know how I was feeling. She was telling me what to do as she was a registered nurse. I gave her the gift; she gave me a hug, and I closed the door. For some reason my unborn child's father was angry that day. He came out of the bedroom and asked me who was at the door. I tried to explain but he got furious. He was fussing at me as he backed me up in a corner. He had his fists raised up as if he was going to hit me. At that moment, I thought of the felony he had, which was for physically attacking someone; he was a trained boxer. I told myself not to talk back or say any trash talk. I calmly asked him to get away from me. I told him, "You're gonna hit me and I just got released from the hospital?" I was six months pregnant at the time of the incident. The day before the incident I had just been released from the hospital. I had to be admitted and watched for a few days due to contractions increasing. Once contractions decreased, I was released to go back home on bed rest.

After about ten minutes, which felt like a lifetime, he backed away. I grabbed my house phone, which was a cordless phone, went to my bedroom and locked myself in the closet. I immediately called my momma, my brothers, and every male friend that I had and told them what happened. Within ten minutes, my brothers and friends had made it to my apartment. He answered the door and they came in. It was a peaceful outcome, thankfully. He packed up his things and they took him to the bus station. One of my friends purchased him a one-way ticket to New Orleans and that was the end of that relationship. He called all day every day for a few weeks crying, apologizing, and trying to get me to take him back, but I could not. I have never been so scared in my life. I had nightmares for a few months about him attacking me while I was pregnant. I had never had a man that I dated or was in a relationship with act as if he was going to hit me or physically hurt me. On top of that, my momma taught me and my older sisters that we should never let a man hit us. Furthermore, I refused to live in fear in my own home. Even though he did not hit me, the fact that he was angry, had me in a corner, and acted like he wanted to hit me was enough for me. I was not and did not take any chances of having a similar situation like that with him. Plus, I had to think of my son and unborn child. None of us were going to live in fear. So, I cried, prayed, and prayed even more, but I never took him back and his calls eventually stopped.

Without income coming in from my employer, I had a decision to make. I no longer had enough money to afford my own place. I knew I could not go stay with my momma as her house had enough people in it. I called local agencies to see where I could get help and even called shelters. However, there was nothing available for me. At that point in time, I had no idea as to what I was going to do. I didn't have solid relationships with other family members to ask if I could stay with them. I didn't feel comfortable asking and I did not want to be a burden to anyone. Finally, a last resort was to call my best friend. I knew she was living in her parents' rental property. I thought maybe I could stay with her just until I got back to work after having the baby. She didn't have a problem with that but said that I needed to speak to her parents about it. I gained the nerve to speak with her mother. By the grace of God, her mother said I could stay there without having to contribute anything. I cried and cried after that telephone conversation. I was extremely grateful and relieved. God had once again answered my prayers.

Eventually, I spoke with the apartment manager and I was released from my lease without penalty. My family members and friends moved me out of my apartment and put all my furniture in storage. I was responsible for making sure I paid my storage fee every month as my belongings would only be there for a few months. I went on to have my second child, another boy, a few months later in May. Then I went back to work in July and moved back into my own place at the end of July. I also registered for school to complete my bachelor's degree that August. I had two children to take care of now. I had to complete my college education to position myself to get a better-paying job.

# Living Life As A Single Parent Of Two

---

**Isaiah 40:31 (KJV)**

*But they that wait upon the LORD shall renew their strength; they shall mount up with wings as eagles; they shall run, and not be weary; and they shall walk, and not faint.*

---

When my second child was about six weeks old, I started dating a new man. A really good male friend of mine called me one day providing details about the guy. He thought he would be a good match for me. I was against meeting the guy because he had the same first name as my oldest son's father and he was younger than me. My friend thought I was being ridiculous and so I agreed to meet him. My friend brought the guy over one evening to my best friend's house and we talked and had drinks. The guy seemed sweet and interested in me. He also accepted the fact that I had two children by two different men with one being a newborn. The evening went well; we exchanged numbers and started talking.

Eventually, we dated and started a relationship. He was an active-duty service member and I had gotten a job on the installation where he worked. So we had lunch together daily, and eventually he moved in with me and my two children. Things were good, but there were bumps along the way. He drank alcohol often and smoked cigarettes. I barely drink alcohol and don't like cigarettes. Despite us being together most of the time, having the same friends and living together, he would get drunk and accuse me of cheating at 1 a.m., 2 a.m., 3 a.m.. He was dealing with some insecurity issues and I tried to reason with him. I would ask him how I could cheat when we were always together. This occurred often.

The year after giving birth to my second child, in that summer, I received my Bachelor of Science degree in Business Management and Administration. I was so excited. I didn't care about attending the graduation in December; all I wanted was the degree. I remembered driving to the school and going to registrar's office during my lunch break, to pick up my diploma. On the way to the school, I called my momma to share the good news with her. My dream of obtaining a college degree had finally been fulfilled.

I thought about all the detours along the way to obtaining my undergraduate degree. First, I left college to run away to the military. After completing my military service, I enrolled back in school. I attended school during the daytime when I worked at night or attended school at night when I worked during the day. The nighttime classes were the roughest because they were three hours long after a long and sometimes stressful day at work. Then, I had to withdraw from school due to a high-risk pregnancy. Despite all that, I endured and never lost focus on my dream; now I had accomplished it. In that moment, I thought of my grandfather. During his last days on Earth, he told me to stay focused, go to college, and get a degree. He died my senior year of high school, right after my graduation. I cried and thanked God over and over. He saw me through.

As soon as I got my diploma, I went back to the installation where my boyfriend worked and showed it to him. I believed he was proud of me. I thanked him for his support and gave him a big hug. He was there helping me out with the children when my family couldn't babysit them. Right then and there, thoughts of pursuing a master's degree ran through my mind. I knew that I wanted to go for it, but I wasn't sure when I was actually going to start.

After I received my bachelor's degree, my boyfriend's attitude changed a little towards me. He would make snide comments saying I thought I was smarter than him. Those things would come out when he was tipsy or drunk. I paid attention to the things he did and said, especially when he was drunk. They really bothered me. I felt like we were a unit. If I was successful, so was he, and vice versa;

that was my way of thinking. However, me obtaining my undergraduate degree made him even more insecure about himself. I never threw my education in his face. However, I did encourage him to enroll in a college class and even offered to help him with his assignments. I was willing to do whatever it took to show him we were a team. I wanted to show him that we were equal; a college degree didn't put me above him.

After about four years of dating, my boyfriend and I decided to have an active church life. He was raised Catholic. We would attend mass every now and then. My children and I would attend other churches occasionally but nothing really routine or even on a weekly basis. One day we got invited to a church by a mutual friend of ours and we decided to go. We had such a really good time at the church we continued to attend weekly. Then we started attending Bible study. We became members and were very active in the church. We attended church as a family every week; that included Sunday, Wednesday night Bible study, Saturday fitness, and attended all special events in or out of town. He converted to Protestantism and was no longer Catholic. He ended up becoming an armor bearer for the pastor.

Along the way, I grew in knowledge of the Lord and His Word. I learned how to pray effectively. I learned about intercessory prayer and the power of praise and worship. I learned about tithing and that tithing is not just money but your time as well. We attended that church for about one year, but in such a short period of time my children and I grew so much spiritually. The men and women of God in that ministry taught me so much. I can honestly say we had fallen in love with the Lord and we were chasing after Him to know more. We had become a part of the ministry and actually enjoyed attending the services and fellowshipping with members.

In January of 2008, I started pursuing a master's degree. I completed it in September of 2010, with a 4.0 grade point average. I was a single parent of two children, working full time, and attending graduate school full time. That has to be one of my proudest moments, besides giving birth to my babies. As soon as I completed my master's, I started applying for higher salary positions within the federal government that required a master's degree.

Unexpectedly, I got a job offer in May of 2011. The job was not just a promotion but also involved relocation to another state, Virginia. My boyfriend and I prayed about the job offer. I went to the pastor of our church and sought prayer as well. Soon after, I received confirmation that I should take the job and I accepted the job offer. Obedience is better than sacrifice. God told me to take the job and I did so, wanting to be obedient and ready for the new opportunity despite knowing that my children and I would be leaving my boyfriend behind.

Well, I had a job offer but had no money to relocate. My boyfriend was able to get a loan and the church blessed me with money to assist with the move as well. Thank God for that. I looked back and realized that by me tithing and giving faithfully, doors were opened for me to be blessed financially so that I could relocate. With those financial blessings, he moved me, the kids, and all my belongings from my hometown in Louisiana to Virginia. We put everything into a U-Haul truck and drove across the country. We moved into the apartment on July 9. My boyfriend set up all the rooms and we were able to get all the boxes unpacked in a day or two. He went back to his installation after getting us settled in. My first day of work was on 1 August 2011.

One day I got a call from my boyfriend stating that he had gotten orders to another military base. I was very happy for him because it was a good assignment, but I was worried about the distance and if we were really going to get married. At this point, I will admit that our relationship was not at its best, but I was trying to make things work because I really loved him. I had invested so much time into him and the relationship that I really did not want to give up on it or him, and more importantly, I did love him, and truly wanted things to work out between us.

Out of the blue, I had a car wreck. I was on my way to pick up my younger child from school and I was hit from behind. My car was totaled and I had to be transported by ambulance. I had been trying to reach my boyfriend but could not reach him. I contacted my momma back in Louisiana and made her aware of what had happened. I contacted my neighbor and told him what happened; he agreed to pick up my younger son. I wasn't able to reach my boyfriend at all. I finally reached him that evening to tell him what had happened. Of course, I was upset because I hadn't been able to reach him. He really gave me no real reason as to why he didn't answer or call me back. Eventually, he told me that he was going to fast for the next seven days and read Deuteronomy because he needed guidance as to what to do about us. I thought nothing of it.

About a week after the car accident and that call, I was driving alone in a rental car and I called my pastor back home in my hometown. I called him to tell him about the wreck and that I had to buy another car. The pastor kept asking me if I was all right. After he asked the third time, I asked him what was going on. The pastor told me that my boyfriend had gotten married last night after Bible Study and he officiated the marriage. He was under the impression that I knew. At first, I thought it was a joke. It was not. I was shocked. I was angry. I was hurt. I was confused. It felt like my heart stopped. Anger took over; I cussed Pastor out and hung up on him. I immediately called my boyfriend; however, he was not answering my calls, or maybe I was blocked. I didn't know what to do but I was in disbelief. I called his closest friend and when he answered the phone he said something like, "I told him you're going to kill him!" He apologized. He really didn't have much to say. I got off the phone in tears and was trying to drive myself home after finding out the love of my life got married to another woman last night in our church after Bible Study.

When I got home, I called everyone back home who attended our church and all our mutual friends. I didn't understand; I needed to get some sort of understanding. Everyone I called verified he was married but insisted they didn't know the woman. Many claimed he had known her for one week before they had gotten married. One person in particular told me to get over it because he was married now and there was nothing I could do. I will never forget her cold response. I spiraled down. I was severely depressed and embarrassed once again. To make things worse, he got married in my hometown. How on Earth was I going to escape this embarrassment? Eventually the pastor called me back; he apologized. He even offered to come to Virginia. I thought, *"What is that going to do?"* I angrily got off the phone. On top of all of that, I called my boyfriend's mother later that evening. She told me she had no idea what her son was doing or who he was married to. She apologized to me for his actions. She told me that my children and I would always be her family. I rudely told her that neither I nor my children could continue to keep in contact with her knowing her son had married another woman and would possibly have children with her. That would be the last time I spoke to her.

All these thoughts went through my head constantly. How could he do this to me? He knew my oldest child's father got married on me without breaking up with me and he did the same thing. Why? Oh Lord, what about my youngest son? My youngest son thinks my boyfriend is his dad. Did he really care about us? How could he do this to us? Is this for real, God? How can this be happening to me again? Am I not worthy to be a wife? Am I cursed?

One night, I was on the floor crying in the dark. I was at an extremely low point. I actually cussed at God. I know I should never have done that. It didn't take long for me to come to my senses and repent repeatedly for that. At that moment, I was so distraught, hurt, and confused. I felt unlovable and unwanted. I remember getting off the floor and going to the living room to sit on the sofa, with an alcoholic beverage on the coffee table. I wanted to give up on life in one thought. Then, I thought of my two baby boys sleeping in the next room, and I knew I could not give up on life or them. I cried and cried and cried. I cried so much I didn't even have a voice. I cut almost everyone off. I only talked to my children because they were there and my next-door neighbor as he knew what was going on.

That following Sunday my momma went to church. She knew he would be there and so she showed up. After church, she respectfully confronted him. She asked him questions I never had an opportunity to ask. My momma asked him how he could do that to me and the kids. She told him flat out that he was wrong in the manner that he handled things. That's all she did. She wanted to let him know that he was wrong and she did just that.

That relationship lasted almost six years. I had hoped that he and I would get married and have children. However, that's not how things played out. I ended up being humiliated and left again. After that break-up, I was at a low point in my life for at least two or three years. I never got any closure. After being with someone all that time, I guess I never really knew him. I was angry at myself; I felt I wasted six years of my life. There was nothing for me to do but move on past the hurt and disappointment. I know I cried at work every day for over a year. I went to work and played gospel music the entire time to help me get through the workday. When I got home, I tried to be upbeat for my children, but it was hard especially when my younger child was asking to talk to a man whom he thought was his father but was not. I could no longer contact him; he was a married man. He was not the father of my baby boy. I tried my best to make sure my children were all right mentally, physically, and spiritually. I began to rely on God even more.

I was hurt by the devastation of the breakup, but it really affected my younger son mentally and emotionally. His entire life he thought this man was his daddy and he walked away from me and my kids. I had to get professional counseling for him. He was having abandonment issues. He wanted to talk to Daddy but I could no longer contact him. I had no idea how to explain to a six-year-old child that Daddy was gone and not coming back. It didn't take long for those issues to negatively affect his behavior in school.

I knew he needed support, so I got him into counseling immediately. There was never any hesitation. It was the best thing I could do for him. It helped him tremendously.

Eventually, one of my coworkers invited me to his church. I was suspicious about attending church because of what had previously happened. I really didn't think I was ready to go to any church. However, my children and I went and we kept on going. We attended Sunday services, Bible Study, and any other service that was happening. My children enjoyed children's church. My youngest son played the congas, then moved to playing the drum set. My oldest son mimed and played his violin occasionally. I sang in the choir and even praise danced. I taught children's church. We participated in most church activities. We tithed and gave offerings faithfully. The entire time I was still broken and hurt and trying to understand the things that had occurred in my life.

In the end, attending that church allowed my children and me to meet some strong spiritual people deeply rooted in God's Word. This church was equivalent to the prior church we had attended back home in Louisiana. God was able to surround me and my children with people who poured into us, uplifted us, encouraged us through the storms, and corrected us when needed. Going to this church allowed me and my children to continue to grow in the things of God and establish a closer relationship with the Lord.

I had received a word before making the decision to take the job in Virginia. I was told that I was holding onto baggage that could not go into my next season. I never really paid attention to it because I didn't think I was holding on to something that should be let go. That revelation would come to me about four years after being left by my boyfriend. It was revealed to me that he could not come with me in that next season. Sometimes God has things that are for you and not for the individuals that you are trying to bring with you. God will remove those individuals that we are so desperately trying to hold on to because we won't let them go ourselves. As hard as it is for me to admit this, my boyfriend marrying someone else turned out to be a blessing in disguise for me as I no longer had to deal with his anger, rage, insecurities, and alcoholism.

So many people have asked me why I dated him for so long. They stated that six years is too long to be dating someone. I probably could have gotten married to that boyfriend sooner; however, I chose not to press the issue. He had issues I have mentioned above. These issues, especially anger and rage, would come to the forefront when he was tipsy or drunk. There were times my boyfriend would be so drunk that he would get my youngest child out of the crib and hold him while he had a loaded gun to his own head, all the while crying. When I first saw my boyfriend do that, it scared the heck out of me. I immediately got my son from him and locked myself and two kids in their room until the next morning. He did that a few more times during our relationship when he got drunk. I knew something had to change before we decided to get married. I knew that I didn't want to be in covenant with any of those things. I hoped that he would quit drinking and control his anger and rage, and then we could get married. Well, that never happened. Instead, God had other plans and allowed that relationship to end.

# Unexpected Blessings While Grieving

---

**Psalm 34:18 (KJV)**

*The LORD is nigh unto them that are of a broken heart; And saveth such as be of a contrite spirit.*

---

Once that relationship ended, I focused on my relationship with God, my children, church, and career. I had no closure from my last relationship. I had a million questions and could not get any answers. Getting close to God was the only way I survived. At night after I tucked the kids into their beds, I cried. There was no one to call. Time had passed and even after a year I was still hurting, asking the Lord, "Why me?" and "Why did that have to happen to me again?" I kept calling friends and pouring my heart out over and over but they eventually got sick and tired of me and my calls. God was the only person I could go to and cry my heart out. I did that at least two or three years after finding out my boyfriend had married another woman.

In my grief at losing the man I loved, I got closer to God. Truth be told, I had to get closer to Him. He was always there for me even at times when I did not think He was. He comforted me always. I was already a lover of Christian and gospel music, but I started to listen to it more and more. Literally, listened to it all day while I was awake unless I was listening to the Bible. I loved singing and I sang all the time. When I hurt and could not pray, I sang a Christian or gospel song. I started listening to the Bible daily. I even played the audible Bible in my home as I cooked our meals and cleaned the house. I played the Bible at night as my kids and I slept. The heartache, pain, and humiliation were all still there, but His words brought me comfort, as well as those Christian and gospel songs since they were rooted in His Word.

Sure, I yearned for companionship, but I was broken and really could not trust anyone. I ensured I was available for my children. We continued to attend church and kept busy with that. As far as work, I wanted a new job. I wanted a promotion, not just any promotion but a financial gain of $25,000 or more a year. I had written a prayer out specifically about the new job I wanted as well as the specific amount of increase in the salary. I didn't want to stay stagnant in my career. I applied for jobs every day once I hit the year mark of being in my current position. My applications were being referred to the hiring manager, but I wasn't receiving any job offers or even calls for interviews. I continued to apply for jobs, and after being at my job for more than four years, I finally got a call.

One day sitting in my office at work, there was a call on my cell phone, but I didn't recognize the number so I didn't answer. I figured it was not important because the caller did not leave a message. A few hours later the cell phone rang again and I answered. It was a gentleman who stated that he was a program manager and he had been trying to reach me for months. I was a little puzzled, as I had not noticed any communication attempts besides his two calls that day. He went on to say that out of about 300 resumes, mine was the only one that contained the qualifications he was looking for. He explained the position and asked me if I was interested in scheduling an interview. I was in shock as he spoke. I thought, out of all those resumes mine was the only one with the desired qualifications. I thought, *"Really, God!?"*

Before I agreed to the interview, he discussed salary. He told me it was a government contract position, with two years left on the contract, and that the salary would range from $90,000 to $110,000. I was totally blown away. I could not believe this was happening to me. I thought, *"Nothing good happens to me."* On top of all of that, it was a job similar to what I was currently doing but at a higher level, improving policies and procedures with a different branch of the military. I thanked God over and over in my head as all this information was being revealed to me. I called my family back home in Louisiana to share the news. I called the leadership at my church and asked them to stand in agreement with me for getting this new job. When I picked up my children from daycare, I told them the good news about the new opportunity. They were just as thankful, happy, and joyful as I was. That night we prayed together as a family, standing in agreement and asking for favor during the interview.

A few days later, after speaking with the project manager, I interviewed for the job. Within a week of interviewing, I was emailed a job offer letter. I did not accept the first offer but instead counteroffered for a $105,000 salary. When I emailed that counteroffer, I regretted sending it. I thought, *I should have just accepted what they offered.* It was way more than the $25,000 increase that I had been praying for. I prayed, praised, and worshipped in my office as I nervously waited for a response. The company emailed me back with a new offer letter with the $105,000 salary that I had asked for. In amazement, I printed out the offer letter, signed it, and sent it back immediately with an acceptance email. I did all of this in disbelief. I had been praying for a new job and a promotion since 2012. I had been very specific in my prayers by stating I desired an increase in salary of $25,000. With my new job, my salary went from around $56,750 to $105,000. That was increase of more than $46,000 in my salary. I was given more than I asked for or even could imagine at that time in my life. I had just hoped for a salary of $75,000 or $80,000. I had never thought about making six figures at that stage in my life. God had other plans for my salary and His plans were clearly higher than mine.

When I picked up my youngest child from daycare, I went straight home. He and I waited for my older child to come home. As soon as he walked through the door, I gave the children the good news. I told them I was starting a new job with a higher salary. They were so happy. I called my family back home in Louisiana and Texas and informed them too. Everyone was so happy for us. That job offer was an unexpected blessing. My children and I had been praying for a few years on our knees at night, specifically praying for a new job with an increased salary. I could not believe that this blessing was bestowed upon me. The Lord answered my prayers beyond what I had asked for. We celebrated by going out to eat.

# Endless Prayer And Praise Through The Valley

---

**Proverbs 3:5-6 (KJV)**

*Trust in the LORD with all thine heart; And lean not unto thine own understanding. In all thy ways acknowledge him, And he shall direct thy paths.*

---

Little did I know I was about to start rolling down the mountaintop. Even though I had a great job as a government contractor, it was about to end abruptly. Soon there was gossip going around the workplace about contracts being cut. I really didn't think about it. However, after about a month of hearing of it, one of my coworkers pulled me aside and asked me if I was looking for federal jobs. He stated that I should start looking and applying. I asked if he knew anything about the chatter concerning contracts being cut, but he didn't answer. I had started looking and applying for a federal government position as soon as I hit my year mark. I wondered about the conversation he and I had as well as the gossip going around at work. Well, within two weeks, three other employees and I were given layoff letters. It turned out that the last four employees hired on the contract were the ones to be laid off. After a year and a half of enjoying a six-figure salary, I had been laid off with barely any notice. I prayed about the situation, but I have to be totally honest; I was worried. My last day of work was June 30. My lease was to end around the 23rd of July.

With my lease about to expire, I had no idea what to do. I immediately started calling family back home in Louisiana and Texas. My family thought it was a blessing in disguise. They felt I moved too far away in the first place and this was an opportunity to move closer. My family told me that they would support me and help me out until I found a new job. I considered the idea; however, I knew my family. I really wasn't too comfortable depending on them. I hate to say this, but one can't always rely on family as sometimes your own family members don't really mean what they say. Also, I wondered if I had actually completed my assignment in Virginia; after all God had sent us there to live.

After careful consideration and prayer, I decided to move to Texas to be closer to my older sisters and their families. Before leaving Virginia, it had been discussed that I would relocate all my furniture to a storage unit in

Texas and my children and I would live with one of my sisters. So, I packed up my apartment, got movers, and moved out of my apartment. I got a storage unit in Texas online. Everything was all set. When my lease ended, I turned in the keys and drove down to Louisiana and then Texas. I didn't know that I was about to go through another one of life's valleys.

I still had an uneasy feeling about the move. However, I didn't pay attention to it. We were really excited about moving closer to family in Louisiana and Texas. I was happy that my sons would be moving closer to their cousins. I felt as if this was a new chapter of our lives and I was open to whatever was coming. Plus, I was excited that the cost of living in Texas was cheaper than Northern Virginia, and thoughts of getting a new job and purchasing a new house danced around in my head.

Unbeknownst to me, I ended up being unemployed for over two years. I was an educated woman with bachelor's and master's degrees but I did not get hired. I applied for hundreds of jobs. I knew in the state of Louisiana or Texas the cost of living was cheaper compared to Virginia. Therefore, I wasn't looking at positions paying a six-figure salary; I was just looking for a job that would pay well enough for me to get my own place and take care of my children. I applied for health care administration jobs in the area. I considered becoming a certified teacher. I applied to become a substitute teacher. I applied for federal government jobs in the local area as well as other cities. I was optimistic. Interview after interview, I still received no job offers. I honestly didn't think I would be unemployed for very long.

My savings started to get extremely low. Credit card bills were racking up. Thankfully, before getting laid off, I had paid my car note off, so I didn't have to worry about that. However, after six months of living with relatives, it was becoming unbearable for me. I thought to myself, *"What have I done wrong?"* I began to pray even more, as well as cry. When I took the children to school, I would go to the local park, sit in the car, cry, pray, and worship for hours every morning. During this valley, I truly didn't understand why I could not obtain a job. I was applying to jobs all day, every day. It had gotten to the point where I was applying for jobs in Louisiana, Texas, and back on the East Coast. I did not limit myself from any jobs. I applied to them all, in several different locations. All I knew was that I had two children that I had to provide for, so I applied for everything.

About six months after being laid off, I began to fast. I fasted every day (seven days a week) for about six to nine months. That fast included fasting from food and television. I ate one meal a day, which was dinner, and nothing after 7 p.m. I fasted in the Word, prayed, worshipped, and drank more water when I could not eat. I was so desperate, desperate to be employed. My sisters could not help me get a job. I didn't know anyone who could pull some strings in Texas to get me employed. The only person I could go to was God. I needed God to move in my life, open doors, or put me in contact with someone who could bless me with a job. I needed Him to give me revelation or guidance as to why I was in that dry place of not getting employed. Day in and day out, I prayed. We went to church every week. I continued to pray, fast, tithe, and give. However, I didn't hear anything from God.

After overstaying my welcome at my oldest sister's house, I decided to move back to my hometown in Louisiana. The decision hurt me to move back home because I never thought I would ever go back. It bothered me because I would have to uproot my children again, to another state this time. However, moving back to my hometown in the state of Louisiana allowed me to have my own place once again. If I had truly considered it when I was first laid off, my children and I would have had our own place. I hadn't realized that I could actually afford a three-bedroom apartment if I had only just moved back to my hometown. I would not realize that until after one year of living with my sisters.

Once I made the decision to move back to my hometown, I immediately started looking for an apartment online Then, I drove down to my hometown so I could actually go see the places that I was interested in. Luckily, I was familiar with the area and knew what schools I wanted my children to attend, so that was key to finding a place to stay in that particular school district. I found the place I wanted; I had income but not enough income needed to actually get the apartment. I reached out to a long-time friend of mine who had his own business and he was willing to provide an employment letter as proof of income. Thankfully, that was all I needed to get the apartment.

After signing the lease in the summer of 2018, my children and I moved in with my momma. It would only be for two months because we could not move into the apartment until our move-in date. I had to enroll the children into school but didn't have an address. I ended up using my cousin's address in order to get my children into the school located in the particular school district that we would be living in. I am so blessed she was willing to allow me to use her address; I had no other options. Sixty days later, my children and I were settled into our apartment, the kids were back in school, and I was still unemployed. Nevertheless, I didn't allow it to get me down. Day in and day out, I applied for jobs online. I used the state of Louisiana job search as well as the federal government job search. I also applied with the school board to be a substitute teacher. I networked with people I knew in town. My friend who assisted me with getting the apartment connected me with an employer. It was a construction company. They needed an office manager only for a short while. I was willing to do whatever it took to take care of my children. I showed up Monday through Friday for a couple of weeks and made about $540.

Once that work was completed, I decided to take the time out to check up on my health concerns with the

Department of Veterans Affairs. I hadn't attempted to seek an increase on my military service disability in years. I really hadn't had the time that was needed to pursue it. Since I wasn't working now and had plenty of time on my hands, I began to follow up on it. I really wasn't expecting anything. I just wanted to initiate the process to see where it would go, if anywhere. Well, I filled out the paperwork and sent it in. Within a few weeks, I attended the medical appointments that were required and just waited. Within three months, I got a letter in the mail. Out of the blue and unexpectedly, I received an increase that was double the amount of what I had been getting. I cried as I read the outcome and saw what my new monthly payment would be. God had given me an increase in a permanent financial blessing. All I could do was thank Him.

Finally, I got an opportunity to interview for a federal government position. The interview was located in Austin, Texas, on 23 July 2019. I accepted the interview without knowing how I was going to get there. I needed money for gas as well as for a hotel room because the interview was at 8:30 a.m. I reached back to my best male friend in Maryland and he sent me $250 without hesitation. I immediately made hotel reservations and prepared for the interview. A few days later, I arrived in Austin and had the interview the following morning. It felt great. When I left the interviewing room, I knew I had gotten the job. I was excited, looking forward to what was going to come next. I consistently prayed for favor to be rested upon my resume and me during the interview. Nightly, I prayed for the Lord to reveal to me if the job was for me.

Seven days later, the night of 30 July 2019, to be exact, I had a dream. I dreamt I was in a conference room at the government agency where I had interviewed. Over an intercom, someone called selectees who were to be hired for positions in two different pay grades. My name was called for one of those positions. When the person speaking was done, he congratulated all the individuals selected and stated that an email would be sent for them to select their duty stations. Then I woke up and wrote that dream down in my personal journal. I was so excited. I thought, *"Has He really revealed that this position is for me?"* I prayed that it was so and remained hopeful.

About a month after interviewing in Austin, Texas, I received an email on 22 August 2019, from the human resource office of the employer. I honestly thought it was a job offer when I saw that the email. Instead, it was an email informing me that while I demonstrated the experience, knowledge, and professionalism required for the position during the interview session, there were more applicants than positions and the initial set of the positions had been filled. My heart dropped. I was so disappointed. Tears rolled down my face. Another door had been closed; at least, that's what I thought. At the end of the email, it stated that they anticipated additional vacancies to open up and they would retain my resume and consider me in the future as positions came available. I had heard that numerous times before  when being considered for a position but it never went anywhere. I honestly didn't know what to expect.

That evening when the boys got home from school, I broke the news to them as we were eating dinner. I tried not to display my disappointment and frustration to them. However, I knew they saw it, sensed it, heard it in my voice, and felt it as well. They both tried to encourage me. In that moment, I truly felt loved and let them know how much I loved them and appreciated them. My kids encouraged me as we rode the storms of life together.

Of course, when they were asleep, I cried my heart out. I contacted my spiritual father. I was angry, upset, sought words of encouragement, and some sort of understanding. After chatting with him, I prayed and cried out unto the Lord. I needed understanding, guidance, and mercy. I truly had a very hard time understanding why I could not obtain a full-time permanent job. I had degrees and over fifteen years of work experience in various areas, but it was out of my reach and I wasn't able to grasp it, or so it seemed.

Soon after, I began substitute teaching. I would continue to work here and there as a teacher, but nothing was permanent. After the new school year started in the fall, I worked at several different schools. However, a month later, I got offered a long-term substitute teaching position at an elementary school that would last until the middle of November. It wasn't my typical work, but I accepted it and

I did it to the best of my ability. I enjoyed being around those kids and it gave me an opportunity to encourage them on their life journey. Through it all, I continued to apply for positions, and I even had a few more interviews.

In October, about a month before the substituting job would end, I got an email to schedule a teleconference interview with another federal government agency in Washington DC. At first, I was hesitant to interview because it was a secretarial position. I hadn't done that in years and I knew I was overqualified for that position. Second, the salary was low considering the cost of living for that area. However, it was a full-time job with full benefits. So, I decided to interview because it was something permanent and I could always climb back up the career ladder. I interviewed for the position and as usual the interview went great. I had a feeling that I was going to be offered the position after I completed the interview. However, I didn't want to get my hopes up too high and be devastated again.

Despite praying, I constantly worried. I wanted to be gainfully employed. I needed to be able to take care of my children. On top of that, my oldest son was a senior in high school; I worried about homecoming, prom, aptitude tests, graduation, and college application fees. I was supposed to purchase him a car during his high school years. I wasn't in a position to do that and that cut me deep. I felt my children were suffering because of me. I really could not understand why after so many interviews there were still no job offers. I even had a Louisiana senator in my corner trying to get me employed at a local hospital, but he, too, was unsuccessful. Through it all, I continued to pray, praise, worship, fast, and apply for jobs when I was not working as a substitute teacher.

# Answered Prayers And Relocation

---

**Hebrews 11:6 (KJV)**

*But without faith it is impossible to please him: for he that cometh to God must believe that he is, and that he is a rewarder of them that diligently seek him.*

---

As time went on, I continued to apply for jobs. I tried to stay optimistic. I read my Bible more than ever when I was unemployed. I bombarded the throne of God with my prayers. I continued to tithe and give even on a limited income during my entire time of being unemployed. I continued to press forward even though it was hard to do at times. Then there was a turn in the tide. On 25 September 2019, I received a job offer from the federal government agency that had not hired me in August but put me on a qualified candidate list. After reading the email, I immediately thought of the dream back in July. I was offered the job at the same pay grade that I had in my dream. I was in awe and amazed. The Lord had revealed it to me back in July and it finally came to pass. A few weeks later I was offered another job. On 15 October 2019, I received a job offer in my email for the secretarial position that I had interviewed for. I had two positions to choose from and both jobs were on the East Coast, located in the area where my children and I had moved from in 2017.

There really wasn't much for me to consider. The position that the Lord had revealed to me in my dream was the position that I was going to accept. I prayed for it to be revealed, He revealed it, and I was not going to be foolish enough to reject the offer. On top of that, the job He revealed to me had the higher salary, a salary that was higher than my last salary that I had in 2017 when I was gainfully employed as a federal government contractor. I was overjoyed. Tears of joy flowed endlessly. After almost two and a half years of not having permanent work, once again, He came through for me.

Immediately, I accepted the job offer that the Lord revealed to me. Within a few weeks, I received a start date of 6 Jan 2020. I had less than two months to relocate for the new position. I started doing research to determine exactly where I was going to relocate in the Washington D.C, Virginia, Maryland area. I had to determine how I was going to relocate myself and my children from Louisiana to the East Coast. On top of that, I had no money available for relocation. I was barely handling my monthly commitments with the income I had coming in. I prayed and sought counsel from my spiritual father.

While fasting and praying, I continued to research where to relocate on the East Coast. The position would be in Maryland but I decided to look for a place to stay in Virginia. I knew the schools were good in all of Virginia, but I decided to look further north where the schools would be even better. After about two weeks of searching for rental properties online, I was able to find a townhouse that suited our needs in a really good neighborhood and excellent school district. Now, I still didn't have any money for relocation nor the deposit on the townhouse.

After a while, I started to feel sick. I finally had a job but I didn't have the means and resources to relocate and secure a place for myself and my children. I really didn't like asking for help from anyone and definitely not asking anyone to borrow money. I knew that everyone was not like me. I would help someone out and not expect anything in return or want anything back. Luckily, I kept in touch with a mentor way back from my high school days. She was actually the reason for me attending all those pre-college programs while I was in high school. I had always admired her and was blessed to have been given the opportunity to participate in those programs. She was aware of me being laid off and not being able to become gainfully employed.

So, I reached out to her and gave her the good news about the job offer, but then I had to ask for a loan at the same time. I was taking a huge leap of faith. I was very hesitant in contacting her. I had never borrowed money from her, not to mention the amount that I was asking for and not really giving any notice or heads up actually made me dizzy. I didn't think that I would obtain the money I needed to relocate for the job. However, I truly believe He led me to contact her. By the grace of God, she was able to loan me the money needed for the U-Haul, gas, and to secure the townhouse for my children and me. God had done it again. He was on roll! He was answering my prayers finally! After two and a half years, my prayers were being answered. I thanked her and Him! Of course, I cried and praised Him!

As soon as she got the funds to me, I rented the U-Haul, secured the place, and started packing. My children and I were looking forward to the new chapter of our lives. The past two and a half years had been rough on us so we were looking forward to a new beginning. The day we were supposed to leave Louisiana driving to the Virginia, I received some disturbing news. I had been busy all that day moving out of the apartment and loading up the U-Haul truck. The guy that was supposed to drive the U-Haul truck to Virginia called me around 4 p.m. and said that he could not drive the truck because he would not make it back in time for work. My heart stopped. My blood pressure skyrocketed. We were supposed to be leaving in eight hours, at midnight. Why did he wait until then to tell me that he would not be able to drive the U-Haul? I was very angry and upset. I told him that I was upset and inquired why he waited so late to tell me. He had no excuses.

Now, I had to scramble to find someone to drive the U-Haul to Virginia. I was driving my car with the kids. I desperately needed someone to drive the U-Haul. I called every person that I knew in my hometown. It was hard to find a driver because it was during the middle of the week and they already had jobs. I upped the ante by offering $500 dollars cash in order to get someone to drive the U-Haul one way to Virginia. There were no takers. Everyone either had other things going on or didn't really want to take that seventeen and a half hour long drive. My last option was to ask my younger brother. I knew he had driven long hours when he resided in Georgia. I truly was afraid to ask because I assumed he would decline my offer. I called my momma and told her that I was going to ask him. I asked her to talk to him and encourage him to help me. She agreed. I put my fears aside and I asked him. Thankfully, he agreed, and my mind was at ease. We left two days behind schedule, but I didn't even care. My children and I were finally on our way to begin new adventures.

# Getting Closer To Him

---

**James 4:8 (KJV)**

*Draw nigh to God, and he will draw nigh to you.*
*Cleanse your hands, ye sinners; and purify*
*your hearts, ye double minded.*

---

Through the years, I experienced many different situations. Some were good and some were not. As I got older and continued to go through various trials and tribulations, I began to seek the Lord. I wanted to get closer to Him. At times, I felt as if the things I went through were actually sent my way to draw me closer to Him.

For many, they have family or friends to confide in and discuss the issues they are facing. For me, it was hard for me to confide in anyone pertaining to the issues I was facing in my past relationships or anything else, for that matter. I was ashamed of the fact that my relationships had problems. Now, I am aware no relationship is perfect and there will be roadblocks or barriers to remove. Back then, that shame caused me to withdraw from others. I was never comfortable speaking to anyone. So for a very a long time, I endured by myself. Then, when I started chasing after God, I took all my cares and concerns to Him. Eventually, I learned to open up and not isolate myself, because that's what the devil wants. The devil wants to isolate everyone and make us feel as if we are alone.

It sounds as if it was easy for me to do. Let me be transparent; it was not. It was a very difficult journey. It took me years to totally rely on Him and find peace in trusting Him. There was a time when I was a lukewarm Christian. I say I was a lukewarm Christian because I allowed the things that occurred in my life to make me doubt the Lord or not trust in Him completely. For example, if problems occurred in my relationship after enjoying a period of bliss, I would start to doubt God and His faithfulness. So, one day I would be chasing after Him full throttle, but a few days later if something went wrong, I would be hesitant about pursuing Him.

At times, I even doubted if He actually heard my prayers. For a long time, I felt my prayers were not reaching Him. I thought others' prayers were being heard and answered, but not mine. I even felt I was wasting my time praying. Out of frustration, I used to say those things to myself out loud, not realizing that my words had power. Even still, I continued to pray.

When I decided to chase Him completely and wholeheartedly, I was no longer lukewarm. God sent several people, including spiritual leaders, in my life to teach me, correct me, love me in spite of who I was, and show me God was and is faithful even when we are not faithful to Him. When I said those things concerning my doubts about God, those people were there to correct me on the spot without hesitation. Through those instances of being corrected, I learned that the Word of God says life and death are in the power of the tongue, which is in Proverbs 18:21. Those people truly cared about me and the things I was going through. However, more importantly, they cared about me and my relationship with the Lord. They all wanted me to get in His Word, to know more about Him for myself, and to get to a place where I knew who I was in Him and who He was.

It took more than a decade to get to that place. I would honestly have to say that it has taken me my entire life to get to the point where I totally trust and have faith in my Lord and Savior Jesus Christ. All the things that I have experienced have made me the woman, child of God, and servant I am today. Today, no matter what the situation looks like, I pray and praise knowing that He hears me. I fully trust Him.

If a negative thought enters in my mind, I pull it down immediately. I didn't use to do that. I used to allow those negative thoughts to have a party and wreak havoc in my mind. Once I learned that there is power in my spoken words, those negative thoughts had to go. So, now I choose to proclaim the opposite of any negative thought that tries to enter my mind. For extra protection of my mind, I recite scripture to cast down negative thoughts. It took me years to learn to do that, but it is my weapon and I will never stop using it. I know the devil is mad, and I am totally fine with that. It has taken a very long time to get where I am today, but I have to say I am truly blessed to be where I am. I used to compare my spiritual journey with others', and I should have never done so. Everyone's spiritual journey is different and unique to each individual person. We all face different things at different times in our lives. I truly believe I am at the beginning of my Christian journey and that I have a much longer journey to go.

# Courage To Share

---

**Joshua 1:9 (KJV)**

*Have not I commanded thee? Be strong and of
a good courage; be not afraid, neither be thou
dismayed: for the LORD thy God is with thee
whithersoever thou goest.*

---

For almost twelve years, I have gone back and forth
about whether or not to share my testimony. Twelve years
ago, I know I could not have written this book. It was not
even an option for me, and I didn't want to even discuss it
nor think about it. I was really scared about sharing some
of the things that I endured. I had been too hurt, ashamed,
and embarrassed to share my experiences. I did not want
to expose all the hurt I had endured. Thinking with my
carnal mind, I thought others would cast judgment on me
and my experiences. In all honesty, I was still hurt and
really hadn't addressed the trauma I endured as a child nor
the painful relationships.

As time passed and I began to heal from my last

relationship that ended in 2012, I have not only gotten older but also my walk with my Lord and Savior Jesus Christ has gotten stronger. At that time, I made the decision not to date or be in a relationship. I chose to focus on my children, myself, and my relationship with the Lord. I really didn't expect to be single for over a decade. I knew I wanted to learn how to love myself and reflect on my actions that possibly played a part in the demise of my relationship. I also had to forgive those that hurt me in the past. I no longer wanted to harbor any unforgiveness in my heart. That took time; specifically, it has taken years. That forgiveness did not happen overnight. I was extremely bitter about the outcomes of my relationships. I had to let go of that bitterness and learn to forgive.

Eventually, I would have to seek professional help from a therapist. The traumatic memories of my childhood experiences and the attack while I was on active duty came to the surface within the past few years. All those memories had been buried and dormant for over two decades. I knew that I had to face the memories and deal with those feelings that were there in order to heal myself and forgive others. It was not easy. It still is not easy, as I am currently addressing those issues today.

During my time of being single and self-reflection, I realized that He had always been with me. It took me a long time to realize that fact. My journey has been long and rough, but as I have thought about past events in my life, all the trials and tribulations, I could actually see where

He had been protecting me even though I did not know it or even see it at that time.

As my relationship with the Lord has gotten stronger, I want to fully walk in my purpose. That was hindered in the past because I was afraid and worried about others' opinions of me. I know that fear is a trick of the enemy. God has not given me a spirit of fear, but of power, love, and a sound mind. That's what 2 Timothy 1:7 says. Once I got that scripture rooted in my mind and heart, I was then able to open up. It was by no means easy; there is still a little hesitation there, but I realize that this is bigger than me. My life and experiences can be beneficial to someone else. It literally took over a decade for me to be in the place where I am today. I know that sharing my testimony and letting others know the goodness of the Lord and the things He has gotten me through can bring about healing as well as possibly lead others to salvation.

To be clear, I want everyone to know that they are not alone. I want others to know about some of my highs and lows, trials and tribulations as well as the obstacles that I overcame. Through all of it, I got through it. Please know that I did not get through it on my own. There was some divine intervention all along the way. Today, I know without a doubt that He was there. He was there leading me, holding me, carrying me, and at times, dragging me. Many of the things I endured some people may not have been able to handle and they probably would have given up on life. There have been a few times along my journey of life where I was at that point and wanted to give up. I just thank God that I had and still have my children as well as my salvation to live for. I didn't want to abandon my children, nor did I want to take the easy way out. I chose to cling onto my faith, believing God has something better in store for me and my children. I know that if He can get me through all the things I have experienced, He can do the same for you. Just seek Him. I promise you won't regret it.

Milton Keynes UK
Ingram Content Group UK Ltd.
UKHW030655120324
439302UK00015B/902

9 798890 414892